Soccer Positions:

A Step-by-Step Guide about Each Player on a Team

Dylan Joseph

Soccer Positions:
A Step-by-Step Guide about Each Player on a Team

By: Dylan Joseph
© 2019

WAIT!

Wouldn't it be nice to have the steps in this book on an easy one-page printout for you to take to the field? Well, here is your chance!

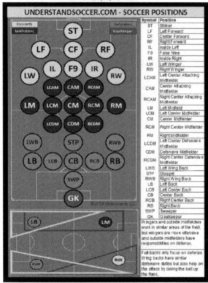

Go to this Link for an **Instant** One-Page Printout:
UnderstandSoccer.com/free-printout

This FREE guide is simply a thank you for purchasing this book. This one-page printout will ensure that the knowledge you obtain from this book makes it to the field.

Table of Contents

Dedication

This book is dedicated to all the soccer players, coaches, and parents who are reading this book to improve their knowledge and strengthen others around them. Whether it is for yourself, your team, or your child; growing to help others and yourself develop is exceptionally noble and speaks volumes about the person you are.

Also, this book is dedicated to all coaches and players who have come before us to lay the foundation for the current tactics and positioning used in the sport today. The complex understandings could have only been made possible by those who have given a significant amount of time to this sport to continually see it develop. For them, I am thankful.

Preface

Great soccer players know the responsibilities of their position. Each position requires players to develop different abilities, and each position has its own strengths and weaknesses. Understanding the position that you want to play—or the role you are already playing—will make it easier to know exactly what to work on and learn. This book gives you the tips, tricks, tweaks, and techniques to become the person on your team who understands each role and can help your teammates develop their skills for their individual positions.

Changing one or two things may help you become better but making learning a life-long goal will allow you to become the player or coach you have always wanted to be. However, remember that the knowledge in this book is only helpful when applied. Therefore, apply it to be sure you are positioned properly on your team.

INDIVIDUAL SOCCER PLAYER'S PYRAMID

If you are looking to improve your skills, your child's confidence, or your players' abilities, then it is essential to understand where this book fits into the bigger picture of developing a soccer player. In the image, the most critical field-specific skills to work on are at the base of the Individual Soccer Player's Pyramid. The pyramid is a quality outline to improve an individual soccer player's game. All the elements in the pyramid and the items surrounding it play a meaningful part in becoming a better player, but certain skills should be read and mastered first before moving on to the others.

You will notice that passing and receiving is at the foundation of the pyramid. This is because if you can receive and make a pass in soccer, then you will be a useful teammate. Even though you may not consistently score, dispossess the other team, or dribble through several opponents, you will still have the fundamental tools needed to play the sport and contribute to your team.

As you move one layer up, you will find yourself needing to decide how to progress. Specifically, the pyramid is created with you in mind because each soccer player and each soccer position has different needs. Therefore, choosing which path to take first is dictated by the position you play—and more importantly, by the position you *want* to play. In soccer and in life, just because you are in a particular spot, position, or even a job does not mean that you have to stay there forever if that is not what you want. However, it is not recommended to refuse to play a position if you are not in the exact role you want. It takes time to develop the skills that will allow you to make a shift from one position to another.

If you want to become a forward, then consider starting your route on the second layer of the pyramid with shooting and finishing. As your abilities to shoot increase, your coach will notice your new finishing skills and will be more likely to move you up the field to an attacking position (if they have not done so already). Be sure to communicate to the coach that you desire to be moved up the field to a more offensive position, which will increase your chances, as well. If you are already a forward, then dive deep into this topic to ensure that you become the leading scorer; first on your team, and then in the entire league. Notice that shooting and finishing is considered less critical than passing and receiving. This is because you have to pass the ball up the field before you can take a shot on net.

Otherwise, you can start by progressing from passing and receiving to dribbling and foot skills because the proper technique is crucial to dribble the ball well. It is often necessary for a soccer player to use a skill to protect the ball from the other team or to advance the ball up the field and place their team in a favorable situation to score. The selection of this route is often taken first by midfielders and occasionally by forwards.

You can also proceed from passing and receiving to defending. Keeping the other team off the scoreboard is not an easy task. Developing a defender's mindset, learning which way to push a forward, understanding how to position your body, knowing when to foul, and using the correct form for headers is critical to a defender on the back line who wants to prevent goals.

Finish all three areas in the second layer of the pyramid before progressing up the pyramid. Dribbling and defending the ball (not just shooting) are useful for an attacker; shooting and defending (not just dribbling) are helpful for a midfielder; while shooting and dribbling (not just defending) are helpful for a defender. Having well-rounded knowledge of the skills needed for the different positions is important for all soccer players. It is especially essential for those soccer players who are looking to change positions in the future. Shooting and finishing, dribbling and foot skills, and defending are oftentimes more beneficial for soccer players to learn first, so focus on these before spending time on the upper areas of the pyramid. In addition, reading about each of these areas will help you better understand what your opponent wants to do.

Once you have improved your skills in the first and second tiers of the pyramid, move up to fitness. It is difficult to go through a passing/dribbling/finishing drill for a few minutes without being out of breath. However, as you practice everything below the fitness category in the pyramid, your fitness and strength will naturally increase. Performing technical drills will allow soccer players to increase their fitness naturally. This will reduce the need to focus exclusively on running for fitness.

Coming from the perspective of both a soccer player and a trainer, I know that constantly focusing on running is not as fulfilling and does not create long-lasting improvements, whereas emphasizing shooting capabilities, foot skills, and defending knowledge creates long-lasting change. Often, coaches who focus on running their players in practice are also coaches who want to improve their team but have limited knowledge of many of the soccer-specific topics that would quickly increase their players' abilities. Not only does fitness in soccer include your endurance; it also addresses your ability to run with agility and speed and to develop strength and power, while using stretching to improve your flexibility. All these tools put together leads to a well-rounded soccer player.

Similar to the tier below it, you should focus on the fitness areas that will help you specifically, while keeping all the topics in mind. For example, you may be a smaller soccer player who could use some size. In this case, you should emphasize weight training so that you can gain the muscle needed to avoid being pushed off the ball. However, you should still stretch before and after a lifting workout or soccer practice/game to ensure that you stay limber and flexible to recover quickly and avoid injuries.

Maybe you are a soccer player in your 20s, 30s, or 40s. In this case, emphasizing your flexibility would do a world of good to ensure that you can keep playing soccer for many more years. However, doing a few sets of push-ups, pull-ups, squats, lunges, sit-ups, etc. per week will help you maintain or gain a desirable physique.

Furthermore, you may be in the prime of your career in high school, college, or at the pro level, which means that obtaining the speed and endurance needed to run for 90+ minutes is the most essential key to continue pursuing your soccer aspirations.

Finally, we travel to the top of the pyramid, which involves tryouts. Although tryouts occur only 1-2 times per year, they have a huge impact on whether you will make the team or be left out of the lineup. Tryouts can cause intense anxiety if you do not know the keys to make sure that you stand out from your competitors and are very confident from the start.

If you have not read the *Understand Soccer* series book, *Soccer Training*, it is highly recommended that you do so to gain general knowledge of crucial topics within the areas of the pyramid. This book will act as a good gauge to see how much you know about each topic, which will help determine if an *Understand Soccer* series book written about a specific subject in the soccer pyramid will be beneficial for you.

The last portion of the pyramid are the areas that surround it. Although these are not skills and topics that can be addressed by your physical abilities, they each play key roles in rounding out a complete soccer player. For example, having a supportive parent/guardian or two is beneficial, as they can provide transportation to games, necessary equipment, team fees, expenses for individual training, and most importantly, encouragement. Having a quality coach, whose teachings and drills will help the individual learn how their performance and skills fit into the team's bigger picture, will help a lot, too.

Obtaining enough restful sleep is critical to have the needed energy during practices and on game days, in addition to recovering from training and games. Appropriate soccer nutrition will increase a soccer player's energy and endurance, help them achieve the ideal physique, and significantly aid their recovery.

Understanding soccer positions will help you determine if a specific role is well-suited for your skills. It is important to know that there are additional types of specific positions—not just forwards, midfielders, and defenders. A former or current professional player in the same position as you can provide guidance on the requirements to effectively play that position.

Finally, you must develop a mindset that will leave you unshakable. This mindset will help you prepare for game situations, learn how to deal with other players, and be mentally tough enough to not worry about circumstances that you cannot control, such as the type of field you play on, the officiating, or the weather.

The pyramid is a great visual aid to consider when choosing which areas to focus on next as a soccer player, coach, or parent. However, remember that a team's pyramid may look slightly different, based on which tactics the players can handle, and which approach the coach decides to use for games.

Now that you know where this book plays into the bigger picture, let us begin.

Remember that if there are any words or terms whose meaning you are unsure of; you can feel free to reference the glossary at the back of the book.

Finally, if you enjoy this book, please leave a review on Amazon to let me know.

Introduction

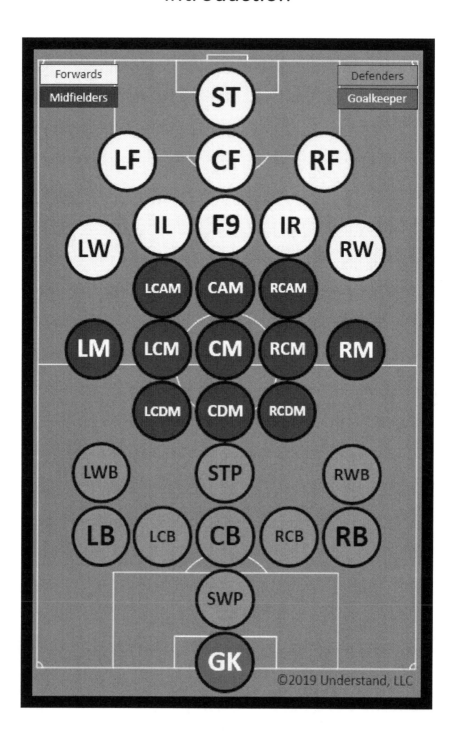

©2019 Understand, LLC

The image details all the possible positions that a coach can assign to a player. Although it may seem overwhelming at first, remember that there are only 11 players on the field, and most formations will never use many of the positions shown. However, I have included them to provide a complete picture of all the options.

GK   Goalkeeper

SWP   Sweeper

RB   Right Back

RCB   Right Center Back

CB   Center Back

LCB   Left Center Back

LB   Left Back

RWB   Right Wing Back

STP   Stopper

LWB   Left Wing Back

RCDM Right Center Defensive Midfielder

CDM   Center Defensive Midfielder

LCDM Left Center Defensive Midfielder

RM   Right Midfielder

RCM   Right Center Midfielder

CM   Center Midfielder

LCM   Left Center Midfielder

LM   Left Midfielder

RCAM Right Center Attacking Midfielder

CAM Center Attacking Midfielder

LCAM Left Center Attacking Midfielder

RW Right Winger

LW Left Winger

IR Inside Right

F9 False Nine

IL Inside Left

RF Right Forward

CF Center Forward

LF Left Forward

ST Striker

This book was written to help the reader understand each position's advantages and disadvantages. Although soccer positions are constantly evolving, this book will help a soccer player determine which position their skills would be best suited for, or which skills they need to develop to play their desired position. This book will also help coaches select which types of roles they want their players to fill, so they can get the most from each player on the team. Keep in mind that positions take on different roles, depending on the strategies and formations used by the coach.

If you are interested in several detailed chapters on all the different formations, as well as their variations, then grab a copy of the *Understand Soccer* series book, **Soccer Coaching: A Step-by-Step Guide on How to Lead Your Players, Manage Parents, and Select the Best Soccer Formation**. This book will help you understand that there are three main formations in today's modern game. Think of these formations as the "Big Three" formations (i.e., 4-4-2, 4-5-1, and 4-3-3).

4-4-2 Formation

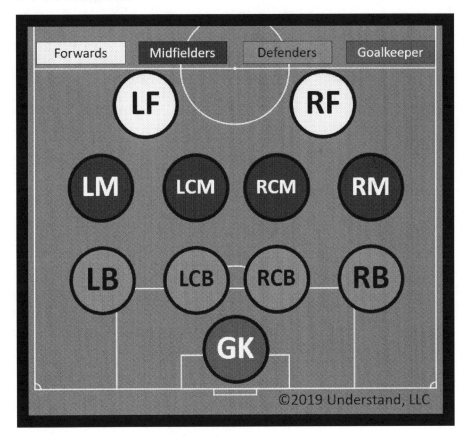

5-4-1 Formation

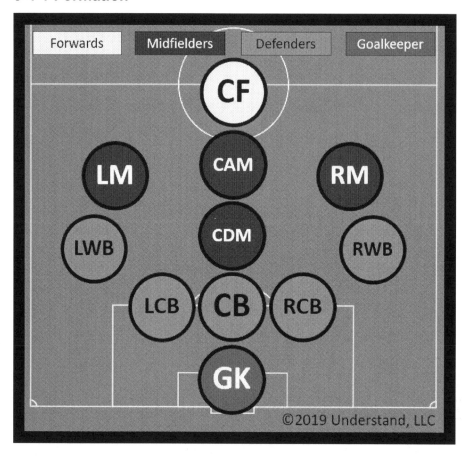

4-3-3 Formation

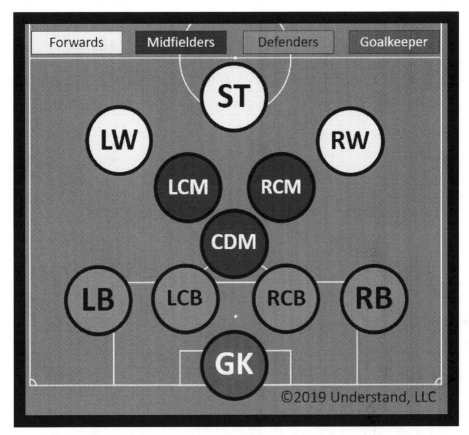

A good coach will assess their players' skills and their team's abilities against other teams. **A knowledgeable coach will know that forcing a preferred formation on a team that cannot handle it is a recipe for disaster. Understand that a great coach will pick their formation based on their players**, and not the other way around. Teams with very skilled players tend to want more forwards and favor the 4-3-3, whereas teams with fewer technical skills and good defenders will benefit from a 5-4-1.

Each chapter in this book, Soccer Positions, will recommend additional books in the *Understand Soccer* series for players or coaches who are seeking more instruction on the skills needed for success. Also, this book will provide outstanding examples of players and coaches whom you should watch and emulate if you would like to succeed in your desired position.

4-3-3 Formation with Player Jersey Numbers

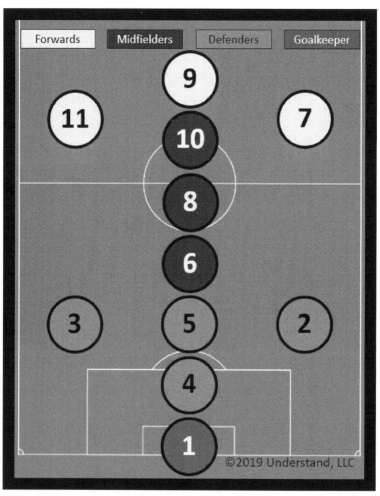

Often, when watching soccer, you will hear the commentator referencing different types of players as "numbers." Although not all teams use it, the standard numbering system for each position started in the 1920s. Numbering each player will help teach those who are still learning about soccer by creating an organized system in which to reference each player. In the image, the jersey numbers are shown using a 4-3-3 formation.

Lastly, this book, *Soccer Positions*, will reveal the traditional number for each player in each position on an 11-player team. Understand that a player's number is not limited to a certain position. A coach can place any number in any position they choose, and each position has different responsibilities to help the team win.

Please reference the glossary near the end of the book for definitions of words with which you are unfamiliar.

Chapter 1

Goalkeeper

Jersey Number: #1

The goalkeeper (also known as the "goalie" or "keeper") controls the 18-yard box, redirects or catches crosses, and prevents the other team from scoring. Goalkeepers wear a different-colored jersey than their team, the opposing team, and the officials. Common colors for a goalkeeper's jersey are black, blue, green, grey, and yellow. They often wear long-sleeved jerseys to protect their arms when diving for the ball, and pants with extra padding made for the position. Since the 1970s, goalkeepers have typically worn gloves to increase the size of their hands, prevent injuries to their hands from powerful shots, and make it easier to catch the ball and punch the ball out of the 18-yard box.

Goalkeepers are the only players on the team who are allowed to use their hands and arms to block shots and pick up the ball while it's in play. The advantage of using their hands only applies in their 18-yard box. Also, they cannot use their hands if a teammate used their feet to intentionally pass the ball to them during gameplay or a throw-in. If all other things are equal, then taller goalkeepers have a slight advantage because they can reach farther and cover more of the net.

The goalkeeper is the most defensive position in soccer because if a goalkeeper does not allow the ball into their net, their team cannot lose. Additionally, when the ball is in the goalkeeper's half, they have increased responsibilities to communicate with and direct their team to prevent the opposition from scoring. This can be while the ball is in play or during a set-piece for the other team.

A traditional goalkeeper (also known as a "shot-stopper") only focuses on preventing the ball from going into their net. They have great reflexes, quick instincts, and considerable agility. They have a limited role when it comes to being a part of attacks and often boot the ball down the field when it rolls to them to keep the ball safely out of their 18-yard box.

Considering the offside rule, having a defender act as a sweeper may be counterproductive if your team wants to catch the opposing players offside. However, in the last couple of decades, it has become commonplace for goalkeepers to assume the "sweeper" role. Modern goalkeepers are used as the starting point of many attacks. Whether they are throwing the ball up the field, kicking the ball to an open attacker, or passing the ball on the ground to a defender; goalkeepers are now more likely to have responsibilities besides keeping the ball out of the net. A sweeper-keeper (also known as a "sweeping goalkeeper") comes out of the net farther than a traditional keeper to help reduce the angle of a player's shot, to act as another field player to whom the defense can pass to maintain possession, and to prevent scoring opportunities by clearing passes and crosses outside the 18-yard box—and all without using their hands!

Skills Needed:

- Not afraid of a powerful shot
- Fast reaction time
- Can jump and dive repeatedly
- Good hands to catch or redirect the ball
- A powerful and accurate dominant foot to kick the ball far up the field during goal kicks and drop kicks
- Clear communication and a calm attitude
- A short memory when they make a mistake
- Ability to maintain focus in a game—even through long stretches of inactivity

Advantages:

- Wears gloves and is the only player who can use their hands in their 18-yard box (excluding throw-ins)
- Wears a different-colored outfit with more padding, thereby allowing their style and flair to shine
- Usually gets the glory in shutouts and shootouts when their team wins

Disadvantages:

- Takes responsibility for all goals against their team—even when it is not their fault
- Generally, does not receive glory for a win but receives criticism for a loss
- Is the least-transferable position because the skills required for a goalkeeper are significantly different than those required for a field player

Example Players:

Gianluigi Buffon – Paris Saint-Germain, Juventus, and the Italian National Team. Buffon was called up for a record of five FIFA World Cups in 1998, 2002, 2006, 2010, and 2014. He won the 2006 FIFA World Cup in Germany. He also represented Italy at four European Championships, at the 1996 Olympics, and at two FIFA Confederations Cups. He is a goalkeeper with incredible longevity. With an approximately 25-year career, he is someone whose form you should emulate to reduce the wear-and-tear injuries that so many goalkeepers face. His style of play is similar to that of a shot-stopper, as he does not contribute much to his team's offensive attacks.

"I've made a lot of mistakes in my life, but I think that's normal for someone who wants to grow and develop. You will have to overcome plenty of obstacles, and it is normal that you should stumble sometimes."—Gianluigi Buffon

Manuel Neuer - Bayern Munich and the German National Team. Neuer is considered to be the first in the new generation of "sweeper-keepers." He is a goalkeeper who will press up and act as a sweeper when the situation demands it. Additionally, when his team has possession, he is quick to distribute the ball, using techniques developed from playing as a midfielder in practice. Neuer has a plethora of hardware in his trophy cabinet. From Footballer of the Year to Champions League Winner, and from German League Champion to World Cup Winner, Neuer is one of the most decorated goalkeepers of all time.

"Take what's useful, leave out what's useless, and add a bit of yourself!"—Manuel Neuer

Chapter 2

Full Back

Jersey Number: #2 or #3

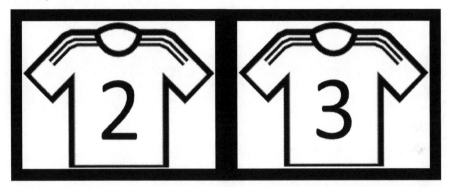

A full back is either the right back (i.e., right defender) or left back (i.e., left defender.) Full backs position themselves to either side of the center backs to limit the effectiveness of wide attackers on the opposing team. They will often cover outside forwards and wingers (depending on the formation used by the other team) to prevent crosses into the 18-yard box and to avoid the ball being dribbled in from the flank (i.e., the field's wide areas.)

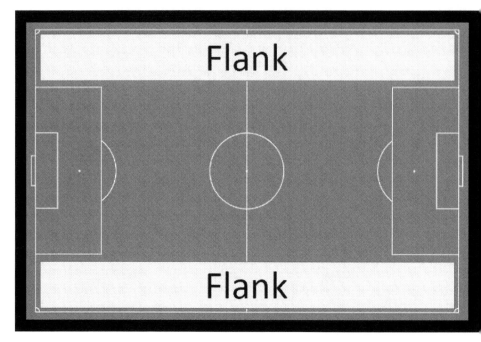

Full backs provide support for the right and left midfielders when they have been beat. They are also another option to pass to when under pressure. Full backs assist with protecting and helping their center backs, too.

Full backs rarely ever join the attack, like a wing back would. Excitingly, full backs are often the players who take throw-ins because they are along the sides of the fields, and coaches want the more skilled midfielders and forwards to receive the ball from a throw-in. Although the midfielders and forwards tend to be better at dribbling the ball, full backs need to be good at passing and receiving because their wide positioning makes them optimal to receive passes.

Full backs need to be fast to keep up with the wingers and outside midfielders on the other team. Although it is not as necessary as it is for a center back, it helps if a full back is also good at heading because they will often need to clear crosses out of their 18-yard box.

It is important that full backs understand how to position themselves in relation to attackers and other players on their team, while still tackling effectively and dispossessing the opposition when needed. Full backs need to understand when to engage the attacking player, and when to reduce pressure, as well. Since center backs and the goalkeeper often have good positions to view the field, they will often shout commands, and the full backs will need to be good at listening to their advice and act on it quickly.

Skills Needed:

- Good at headers
- Can tackle an attacker
- Tracking abilities
- Good at taking directions
- Quick pace

Advantages:

- Focus only on their major role of preventing the other team from scoring, unlike a wing back
- Takes throw-ins
- Often faster than the center backs because they need to shut down the quick wingers and outside midfielders

Disadvantages:

- Few opportunities to score or provide assists
- Wing backs who are more skilled with the ball are more preferred than full backs in today's style of play
- Generally, full backs do not receive the glory for a win but do receive the criticism for a loss

Example Players:

Paolo Maldini - AC Milan and the Italian National Team. Over the course of Maldini's 20+ year career, he has won several Champions Leagues, the Serie A on multiple occasions, and numerous Super Cups, too. He started as a full back and played a considerable amount of his career as a left back—even though he was right-footed—because he was so effective at shutting down the other team's dominant right-footed players. Maldini was so technical that he only made .56 tackles per game—which is unheard of for a defender at his level. He cared about beating the other team by mentally outwitting and out-positioning them, while most other defenders only attempt to overpower the other team.

"If I have to make a tackle, then I have already made a mistake."—Paulo Maldini

<u>Philipp Lahm</u> - Bayern Munich and the German National Team. To gain insight on the leader that Lahm was, consider that, as a defender, he was named captain of Bayern Munich. Bayern Munich has been the most consistent German team over the past two decades, with Philipp Lahm leading the charge for much of that time. Lahm has many of the most coveted trophies in soccer. From being a German Footballer of the Year to a World Cup Winner and Champions League Winner to winning every major trophy in Germany, Philipp Lahm has the winning attitude and drive that a full back needs.

"One of the reasons for my success at Bayern is the relationship with Philipp Lahm; he helped me a lot from the beginning. He always performs. I have never seen Philipp have a poor match. He will always be a special person in my life, and he is an absolute legend. Philipp Lahm is the most intelligent soccer player I have ever coached."—Pep Guardiola

YouTube: If you would like to see a video on the full back position, then consider watching the *Understand Soccer* YouTube video: *Full Back Positioning*.

Chapter 3

Wing Back

Jersey Number: #2 or #3

Note: These are the same numbers as a right full back and left full back.

As one of the most challenging soccer positions, a wing back plays on the sides of the center backs. This placement is similar to that of a full back because a wing back often has the same defensive responsibilities. However, a wing back also contributes to the team's attack. These "attacking full backs" work in the flanks, which is also where wingers can be found. The name "wing back" is a combination of "winger" and "full back."

Wing backs are more adventurous than full backs and can potentially act as the wingers on a team that is without wingers. This position allows for a considerable amount of width when attacking. Width is important to create gaps between defenders and increase the number of passing options. Due to their positioning in the flanks, wing backs must be good at crossing the ball. Wing backs help create coverage gaps because they line up as full backs but attack up the field, thereby making it difficult for opposing teams to decide who will cover them. Consider the below image to further understand the differences in field positioning between a full back (left full back) and a wing back (right wing back).

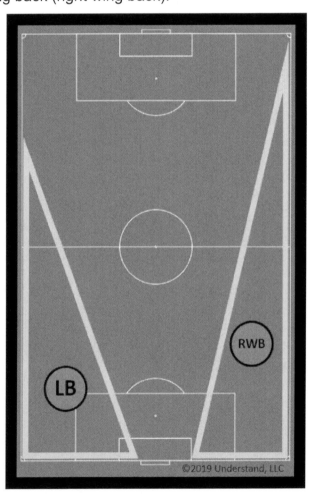

Wing backs must have great endurance because of their offensive and defensive responsibilities in what is one of the most physically demanding positions in modern soccer. However, a quality coach will pick a formation like a 5-3-2, which suits the use of a wing back. Otherwise, the coach may surround the wing back with a holding midfielder and outside midfielder, who can defend and help relieve some of the defensive requirements of a wing back. Wing backs are often a feature of teams who play with three center backs. If a team uses two wing backs, then the wing back on the side with the ball will be permitted to travel up the field and help with the attack, while the other must stay back and defend like a traditional full back.

Skills Needed:

- Can cross the ball into the 18-yard box
- Has a ton of stamina
- Can defend attacking players effectively
- Good at taking directions
- Can dribble at speed to travel past the other team
- Effective at communicating when they need help from teammates

Advantages:

- Focuses on preventing the other team from scoring and helping their team attack by providing assists
- Takes throw-ins
- Often faster than the center backs because they need to shut down the quick wingers and outside midfielders

Disadvantages:

- Must run a ton due to their offensive and defensive responsibilities
- Are often blamed for the other team's goals if they do not get back into a defensive position in time
- Although they are part of the attack, they rarely score because they play in the flanks

Example Players:

Dani Alves - Paris Saint-Germain, Juventus, Barcelona, and the Brazilian National Team. Dani is the definition of a hard worker. As a child, he used to wake up at 4 AM to help his father on the farm, and then he would spend most of the evening soccer training. His family could not afford to let Dani play for a club, so they assembled a team themselves to give him the opportunity to improve. This can-do attitude allowed him to win the Champions League multiple times, as well as the UEFA Cup, and the UEFA Super Cup. Also, he has won the league and cup title of all three major soccer nations he has played in (Spain, Italy, and France.) Alves is seen as an attacker placed in a defensive position. In fact, during his eight years with Barcelona, he had 102 assists as a wing back. That is 10 more assists than the famous attacking midfielder Zinedine Zidane had for both club and country.

"It would be difficult to find another like him."—Lionel Messi, when asked about Dani Alves' departure from Barcelona

Marcelo Vieira - Real Madrid and the Brazilian National Team. Many Brazilians are known only by one name. This is the case for Marcelo Vieira, who is largely known as "Marcelo." Having played for over a decade with Real Madrid and being the starting left wing back for the high-performing Brazilian National Team, Marcelo has been on the big stage all his adult life. However, as a child, Marcelo had no formal education and came from a very rough area. Playing soccer was the only thing he learned during his childhood because the soccer club he played in also doubled as his school. At one point, Marcelo almost had to quit soccer because he could not afford the bus to take him to training. However, his focus and drive helped him find a way onto the local club team before being signed by Real Madrid. Marcelo's never-quit attitude has allowed him to be one of the best wing backs of all-time. His work ethic has helped his team win numerous Champions Leagues, several La Liga titles, the Spanish Cup, and the Confederations Cup.

"The rule is: If you cannot get back [in time to support the defense], you must not go forward. The current best specialist is Marcelo, who gets it right in both areas."—Paolo Maldini

Chapter 4

Sweeper

Jersey Number: #4

The sweeper (also known as the "libero", which is Italian for "free") acts a defender with no marking responsibilities. They line up behind the other defenders and are free to disrupt the opposition however they please. A sweeper acts as a type of center-back who sweeps away the ball if an opponent manages to pass through or dribble past the line of defensive players.

The sweeper has fallen out of favor in recent years, as this position almost always ensures that you cannot catch the other team offsides when you have a roaming defender behind the line of defense. Sweepers are usually faster than other players and must be great at reading the game since they can roam wherever support is needed.

Because a sweeper can take possession of the ball by dispossessing an opposing dribbler—or more commonly, by cutting off a passing lane—they usually need good passing skills to create a quick counterattack. Since a sweeper is behind the other defenders, they often direct their teammates on what to do and who to mark, based on everyone's positioning, and the sweeper's vision of the field.

Skills Needed:

- Great vision and can read the game
- Fast reaction time
- Good defending skills
- Can pass the ball after dispossessing the other team
- Communication and leadership abilities
- Good at judging when to tackle

Advantages:

- Can roam to the portion of the defense where help is needed
- Often starts the counterattack
- Has the best defensive point-of-view, which allows them to direct the defense

Disadvantages:

- A mistake often becomes a goal for the other team
- Generally, they do not receive the glory for a win, but they do receive criticism for a loss
- Often prevents the other team from being caught offside

Example Players:

Franz Beckenbauer - Bayern Munich and the West German National Team. Nicknamed "The Emperor," he was regarded by many as the best sweeper of all-time and is credited with being the originator of this position. Beckenbauer was a two-time winner of the Ballon d'Or Award in 1972 and 1976. He is the only person in soccer history to have both captained and managed World Cup winning teams. He has won the Bundesliga, the UEFA Cup, and the UEFA European Football Championship, among other things. Being the first true libero, he also involved himself in the attack on numerous occasions. In fact, he even scored 14 goals internationally during his career—even though he was the player positioned closest to his own keeper.

"Soccer is one of the world's best means of communication. It is impartial, apolitical, and universal. Soccer unites people around the world every day. Young or old, players

or fans, rich or poor, the game makes everyone equal, stirs the imagination, makes people happy, and makes them sad."—Franz Beckenbauer

<u>Leonardo Bonucci</u> - Juventus and the Italian National Team. Bonucci is an Italian Footballer of the Year, an Italian Super Cup Winner, a Euro 2020 winner, and he has multiple Serie A league titles. In 2012, while browsing in a Ferrari dealership with his wife and son, a man whose face was covered approached Bonucci. He pointed a gun at Bonucci and demanded that the soccer player hand over his watch. Bonucci would have been wise to agree to the assailant's desires, but as the man went to take his watch, Bonucci punched him in the face, knocking him to the floor. Although this was a poor choice, and he would have been better off just handing over his watch, this is an example of his all-out relentless mindset and tough-as-nails character.

"One of my favorite ever players."—Pep Guardiola on Leonardo Bonucci

YouTube: If you would like to see a video on the sweeper position, then consider watching the *Understand Soccer* YouTube video: <u>*Sweeper in Soccer*</u>.

Chapter 5

Center Back/Stopper

Jersey Number: #5

Although in a formation, the "stopper" is positioned slightly in front of a center back, they largely serve the same function, so both will be discussed as one in this chapter. A center back is also referred to as the "center defender" or "center full back." Similar to the goalkeeper, the center back/stopper ensures that the other team does not score. Given that there are often a considerable amount of crosses into the 18-yard box, or clearances by the other team, the center back/stopper benefits from considerable height, size, strength, a high vertical leap, man-marking abilities, and consistency when heading the ball. Therefore, the center back/stopper is often one of the tallest (if not the tallest) players on the team.

Center backs generally use one of two defensive tactics to stop attackers. First, they may use zone coverage, which occurs when each center back handles a specific portion of the backfield. Otherwise, they may use man-to-man marking, which occurs when each center back manages one specific attacker on the other team. The man-to-man marking technique is more common for many soccer teams because it leaves no room for miscommunications regarding who covers each player. The zone-marking tactic requires defenders who can better read the game.

Center backs put their bodies on the line to make it as difficult as possible for the attackers on the opposing team. Center backs often push the boundaries of the game in terms of physical contact and they force the referees to consider making calls to keep the players safe. From hassling and annoying attackers to holding and tripping strikers, they may attempt to slow the other team in ways that are against the rules. Although center defenders will get calls against them, they will continue to frustrate the opposition—especially outside their own 18-yard penalty box.

Traditionally, center backs use to kick the ball up the field to keep it away from their net, but modern center backs often play a pivotal function in maintaining possession or finding passing lanes to midfielders or forwards.

Skills Needed:

- High vertical leap
- Considerable height and size
- Good at headers
- Can tackle an attacker
- Tracking abilities
- Good communication
- Accurate long passes

Advantages:

- A leader who is often the captain of the defense
- Large physical presence makes them difficult to get past in the air
- Frequently involved in the 18-yard box during set pieces and corner kicks on both sides of the field

Disadvantages:

- Takes responsibility for all goals against their team—even when it is not their fault
- Generally, center backs do not receive the glory for a win, but they do receive the criticism for a loss
- Often, they are not the fastest player because of their significant height and size

Example Players:

Giorgio Chiellini – Juventus and the Italian National Team. Chiellini, towering at 6'2", is an Italian superstar and Olympian. Chiellini is a 3X Defender of the Year in Serie A and has multiple league titles as part of Juventus. He recently won the Euro 2020, too. His demanding physical presence has forced forwards to retaliate in other ways to slow his game. From four broken noses to being bitten by Luis Suárez in the 2014 World Cup, Chiellini has taken abuse, as well as regularly dished it out.

"For me, the defender I respect the most is Giorgio Chiellini. He is one of the best defenders in the world. I really like the way he plays soccer on the pitch, the way he defends. He lives for the game. He transmits a sense of tranquility to his teammates. I have always admired his way to play."—Edinson Cavani

Sergio Ramos – Paris Saint-Germain, Real Madrid, and the Spanish National Team. Sergio Ramos is one of the most disliked players in the game. His physical style, in-your-face attitude, and additional ability to score big goals from set pieces in important games has only made the list of folks who dislike him even longer. His background includes amassing about 30 red cards, and in the 2018 Champions League Final, breaking the collarbone of Liverpool's star player, Mohamed Salah. Within days of breaking Mohamed Salah's collarbone, over 500,000 people had signed a petition stating that Ramos was "an awful example to future generations" and urged soccer's governing bodies to punish him retroactively. Although he is not a great role model based on his antics, his abilities to perform when an important game is on the line and to be an overbearing defender in the backfield have allowed him to play for one of the best teams in the world for over a decade. Additionally, he has won a World Cup, multiple Champions Leagues, and about every worthwhile top-flight soccer competition in Spain.

"Nothing fills me more than the feeling of having given everything."—Sergio Ramos

Defending Summary

Defenders need to remember to focus on their main responsibility—specifically, to prevent the other team from scoring. One way to do this is with proper body positioning. **As a defender, your body positioning should be angled.** You should never point (i.e., "square") your hips at the attacker completely, because then it will allow the attacker to go to the right of you, to the left of you, or between your legs. You should be angled but not entirely turned to the side. Position one of your sides so that it faces the attacker but is still at a diagonal. If your feet were hands on a clock, then they should be positioned at either "10 and 4," (as shown in the first image) or "8 and 2," (as shown in the second image.)

This body positioning will allow you to push them either to the left or the right. **Standing at "10 and 4" will push them to their left foot and standing at "8 and 2" will push them to their right foot.** Keep in mind that just standing directly in front of them and turning your hips will not force them in the direction that you want them to go. You must be slightly off-center, with your hips set at either "10 and 4" or "8 and 2," to push them in the direction that you want them to go. If you just turn your hips directly in front of a good dribbler, then they will attack the side that you are not facing, which will make it easier for them to go around you. This will force you to turn farther to pursue them.

The above excerpt from the *Understand Soccer* series book, **Soccer Defending: A Step-by-Step Guide on How to Stop the Other Team**, reveals that it is best to position yourself slightly closer to the side in which you do not want the attacker to go. If they attack in the direction in which you are forcing them to go, then your positioning will make it easier for you to tackle or pursue.

Chapter 6

Defensive/Holding Midfielder

Jersey Number: #6

Originally, midfielders were referred to as "half backs" because half their role was to play defense, and the other half was to play offense. Defensive midfielders are center midfielders who specialize in dispossessing the other team and cutting off passing lanes. Of all the midfield players, the defensive/holding midfielder is often viewed as the "ball winner." A ball winner is a soccer player who focuses on winning the ball back from the other team by intercepting it or making defensive challenges and the occasional tackle. This attribute almost always describes a defender. Putting this label on a midfielder signifies that they are the team's defensive center midfielder (also known as the "pivot").

A defensive midfielder is positioned just behind the center midfielder. Defensive midfielders allow the other center midfielder to focus more on attacking. When their team has the ball, defensive midfielders connect the defense to the midfield by moving the ball from one to the other. When the other team has the ball, they are tasked to prevent the ball from reaching the defense.

Passing and receiving skills are a must since they are in a crowded portion of the field. They must control a pass and distribute it to the open player. Therefore, holding midfielders can also make effective deep-lying playmakers. Deep-lying playmakers are players who position themselves near their team's defense, but because of their strong long-distance passing abilities, they can create quick attacking opportunities by playing the ball past many of the opposing players with just one pass.

Holding midfielders must be good tacklers, great at positioning themselves to cut off passes, and have a significant amount of endurance. Often, holding midfielders push attacking players towards the sidelines of the field to reduce the opposition's chances of creating dangerous plays and scoring. Holding midfielders are required to cover their defensive teammates when they have gone up the field to help the attack, which is often the case if the team uses a wing back. Holding midfielders slow the other team's speed of play and are often required to cover the opposition's best midfield player.

Skills Needed:

- Can tackle an attacker
- Passing and receiving in the part of the field with the most pressure
- Good at taking and giving directions
- Significant endurance
- Can shoot from outside the 18-yard box
- Knows when to commit a tactical foul

Advantages:

- Has mobility and can go wherever the situation demands
- Occasionally provide assists
- Helps prevent counterattacks from the other team

Disadvantages:

- Generally, does not score many goals
- Needs stamina and endurance because they tend to be one of the players who run the most
- Plays in the most congested portion of the field, which prevents much dribbling

Example Players:

N'Golo Kanté - Chelsea, Leicester, and the French National Team. Kanté is a relative newcomer to the soccer scene but has made a tremendous impact in a very short time. He was the engine behind Leicester City's famous title run, a team with 5000:1 odds at the beginning of the season to win the English Premier League. He has won the World Cup, French Footballer of the Year, the FA Cup, and back-to-back EPL titles. His quick rise to soccer stardom has resulted in humorous and untrue statements, known as "Kanté Facts." A few of the best are "the Earth is covered 70% by water, and the rest by Kanté," "Kanté can tackle your imaginary friends," and "Kanté once ran the London Marathon as a warm-up before a game." All these fake but funny quotes help describe the wealth of energy and endurance that Kanté uses in every game.

"This player, Kanté, he was running so hard that I thought he must have a pack full of batteries hidden in his shorts. He never stopped running in training. I tell him, 'One day, I am going to see you cross the ball, and then finish the cross with a header yourself.' He is unbelievable."—Claudio Ranieri

Sergio Busquets – Barcelona and the Spanish National Team. Being a tall and slow player, Busquets was not considered one of the best for many years—until the soccer world finally realized why Pep Guardiola brought him in. He has endurance, intelligence, and no desire to be recognized. One downfall of most holding midfielders is their need to seek the instant adoration and fame from fans when they score goals for their team. However, not playing this role properly forms a void in the midfield that many selfish defensive midfielders have demonstrated. Busquets is uninterested in the public's praise; he is only interested in helping his team win by playing as the best holding midfielder that he can possibly be. Busquets has quite the résumé. He has won the Euros, every meaningful Spanish title imaginable, the World Cup, and the Champions League on multiple occasions.

"I play in a position that demands hard work, and generosity, and little glamour, but I like it. It is my job, and I like it. I would rather intercept and steal 10 balls than shoot. That is what I am here for—to make everyone else's jobs easier."— Sergio Busquets

YouTube: If you would like to see a video on the holding midfielder position, then consider watching the *Understand Soccer* YouTube video: *Defensive Midfielder Positioning*.

Chapter 7

Outside Midfielder

Jersey Number: **Right Midfielder - #7**

Left Midfielder - #11

Traditionally known as a "left half" or "right half," outside midfielders are midfielders positioned to the right and left of the center midfielders. Outside midfielders provide width in the midfield. Width allows them to create space on the field by pulling the opponent's defense to the outside, so they can open lanes for their offense.

Having two outside midfielders, along with two center midfielders, means that the team is defensive-minded and willing to reduce some of their attacking power to prevent the other team from scoring. Conversely, having two wingers, instead of two outside midfielders, means that the team is giving the full backs less defensive support and is instead emphasizing the attack.

An outside midfielder's responsibilities are largely to cross balls into the 18-yard box and prevent the other team's outside midfielders/wing backs from being effective during the opposing team's attack. To shoot or cross the ball into the 18-yard box, one-on-one skills are helpful. However, outside midfielders have less shooting responsibilities. When they do shoot, most of their shots come from the edge of the 18-yard box and from crosses from the other side of the field. Because of outside midfielders' offensive and defensive responsibilities, and because they are in the uncrowded flanks, they will need considerable stamina. Additionally, due to their positioning in the flanks, outside midfielders should be open to and good at receiving directions from other players. They often do not have as good of a view as center midfielders or defenders, so they would be wise to act on the directions of their teammates.

Skills Needed:

- Considerable stamina
- Foot skills to travel past opposing players to cross the ball or shoot
- Effective at crossing the ball into the 18-yard box
- Can defend and close the other team's passing lanes

- A powerful and accurate shot
- Receptive to directions from teammates

Advantages:

- Offensive responsibilities to help their team score, which can result in goals or assists
- Since the outside midfielders work in the flanks, mistakes made by them are unlikely to result directly in a goal
- Great endurance

Disadvantages:

- Must balance defensive and offensive responsibilities, unlike a predominately offensive winger
- Generally, does not have many opportunities with the ball each game, which also limits their chances to score
- Since the flanks have more space than any other portion of the field, a mistake with the ball may result in no nearby teammates who can help win the ball back

Example Players:

Philippe Coutinho – Barcelona, Liverpool, Inter Milan, and the Brazilian National Team. As a Spanish Champion, Italian and Spanish Cup Winner, Under-20 World Cup

Champion, and Italian and Spanish Super Cup Winner, he is a good outside midfielder, who sometimes lines up as a winger, given his abilities to dribble and shoot. Coutinho is a student of the game who understands that becoming better is a process and takes time. He and his two brothers watch and break down each of Philippe's games to help improve his latest performance. This dedication reveals why he has had success in three of the top leagues in Europe.

"I see soccer as a bit like a stairway. You have to climb it bit by bit. First, you have to play good soccer so that you get to play for a good team. Then hopefully, you achieve such a level that you are invited to play for your national side in time for a World Cup."—Philippe Coutinho

David Beckham - LA Galaxy, Paris Saint-Germain, Real Madrid, Manchester United, and the English National Team. For many passive soccer watchers, David Beckham is one of the most recognized names in soccer. Due to his conventional good looks, and his marriage to one of the Spice Girls, he created a huge brand for himself that crossed the barrier between soccer and mainstream media. However, all the media popularity was a result of his nonstop work ethic in soccer. Given that Beckham was an outside midfielder, he became top of the class with his dangerous free kicks and crosses. He could achieve so much curve with the ball that many soccer fans refer to a player who can curve the ball as being able to "bend it like Beckham." His nonstop running and wonderful crosses helped him become a Champions League Winner and the Best Player in Europe. Seemingly, whichever country he went to, he became a champion. This includes England, Spain, France, and even the United States of America. From FA Cups to Super Cups, and even Intercontinental Cups, Beckham has a decorated tenure in professional soccer.

"The only time you run out of chances is when you stop taking them."—David Beckham

Chapter 8

Center/Box-to-Box Midfielder

Jersey Number: #8

A center midfielder is in the middle of the team. Center midfielders are surrounded by the offense and defense of both teams and are shoulder-to-shoulder with the midfielders of the opposing team. Therefore, they must be skilled with the ball in the most congested portion of the field. They have similar scoring responsibilities as an attacking midfielder, and similar goal-preventing responsibilities as a defensive midfielder. They also provide help when defending set pieces and must tackle properly to dispossess the other team. Due to their responsibilities on both sides of the ball, the box-to-box midfielders often have the most endurance of any player on the team.

A center midfielder is an important starting point of attack for a team. Center midfielders tend to be "playmakers" who distribute the ball to the attacking players after having moved it past most of the midfielders and some defenders. It is vital that they have exceptional passing skills and great vision of the field to understand the movements of their teammates and the opposing team.

When attacking, they often take shots from outside the 18-yard box to help their team score. Since a considerable amount of the game occurs in their portion of the field, midfielders often exert the greatest influence over a match. This is because the team that controls the middle third of the field is often the team that wins the game.

Skills Needed:

- Considerable endurance
- Accurate passes
- Excellent first touch
- Can dribble with a considerable amount of pressure
- Control over gameplay and flow
- Can shoot from outside the 18-yard box
- Leadership skills

Advantages:

- Usually handles the ball the most

- Provides many assists
- Usually, they are team leaders and are almost always a part of the play, due to their central position, and their defensive and offensive responsibilities

Disadvantages:

- Needs a considerable amount of endurance to play both defensively and offensively
- Must manage the different personalities of each player on the team
- Often passes the ball before they can shoot

Example Players:

Luka Modrić - Real Madrid, Tottenham, and the Croatian National Team. Modrić was born during the Croatian War of Independence, and although he did not partake in the conflict himself, he had family members whose lives were taken because of it. He attributes his strong work ethic and confidence to being raised in this horrifying experience. This tough-as-nails mentality allowed him to dethrone a decade of Messi and Ronaldo as FIFA Ballon d'Or Winners. Additionally, his outstanding effort and endless stamina allowed him to win the Best Player Award in the 2018 World Cup—even though he was on the losing team in the Finals. From winning the UEFA Best

Player in Europe Award and multiple Player of the Year Awards in Croatia, to several Champions League victories and league titles in Croatia and Spain, he has a high-profile trophy case to contrast his modest and humble personality.

"The most important thing is to never give up, never give in to the circumstances, believe in yourself, and to soldier on, no matter what is in your way."—Luka Modrić

Paul Pogba – Manchester United, Juventus, and the French National Team. Pogba grew up in Paris with two brothers, who now play for the Guinea National Team. All three of them were very competitive and pushed each other to succeed in soccer. Their love for soccer was helped tremendously by their mother, who supported their soccer ambitions. Pogba is known for his pinpoint-accurate passing and flair for the game. These attributes have allowed him to win the World Cup and the Europa League, while attracting a €105M transfer fee in 2016—the largest ever at the time. Furthermore, he has an English League Cup victory, and many Italian trophies to his name.

"I only think about the pitch. I want to do great. I want to be one of the best. I want to win titles. I want to achieve things."—Paul Pogba

YouTube: If you would like to see a video on the center midfielder position, then consider watching the *Understand Soccer* YouTube video: <u>*What is a Box-to-Box Midfielder*</u>.

Chapter 9

Attacking Midfielder

Jersey Number: #10

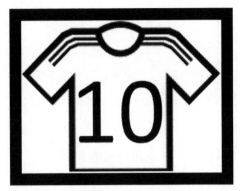

An attacking midfielder is sometimes referred to as the "center attacking midfielder (CAM)," "creative midfielder," or "playmaker." They are stationed ahead of the rest of the midfield and behind the forwards. They tend to act as the main distributor of the ball, the initiator of most attacks, and they are considered by many to be the "soccer coach" on the field. Many soccer fans consider the #10 jersey to be the most prestigious jersey on the field, and it is often given to the best attacking player on the team—sometimes, even when they do not play attacking center midfielder.

An attacking midfielder's primary job is to collect the ball from other midfielders and defenders on the team. Therefore, they must control the pass and take a quality first-touch. The attacking center midfielder looks to where their teammates are positioned—often before they even receive the pass. From there, they judge whether to pass the ball to a teammate who has a better chance of progressing the play or to keep the ball and dribble themselves. Even a well-organized defense can be torn apart with an attacking center midfielder's vision and creativity.

Next, as the play develops, the attacking center midfielder constantly looks for a teammate to pass to, and when nearing the outside of the 18-yard box, they begin to think about shooting the ball, too. The better the attacking center midfielder, the more players from the other team they will draw towards them, thereby creating opportunities for their teammates to score. Due to their positioning on the field, attacking center midfielders and center forwards are often said to be "playing in the hole" of the opposing team's defense.

Attacking midfielders are often allowed a great deal of freedom to travel where they deem appropriate on the field. Their shifty movements can make it difficult for defenders to mark everyone appropriately, thereby creating havoc for the other team. All these responsibilities mean that attacking midfielders need to have strong stamina.

Additionally, an attacking midfielder may act as a second striker. In this role, the attacking midfielder acts as a supporting striker who can both score goals and distribute the ball to teammates who are making a run.

When a team uses an attacking center midfielder, they are usually paired with a defensive midfielder who focuses on preventing the other team from scoring. You will rarely see a player positioned as a false nine (discussed in a later chapter), an attacking midfielder, and a center midfielder on the same team.

Remember, the attacking midfielder is still a part of the midfield, and therefore they must have some defensive responsibilities. They must look to cut off passing lanes through the most dangerous part of the field—the middle. Attacking midfielders also need to position themselves well to prevent the other team from using their midfielders to start attacks.

Skills Needed:

- Can shoot from outside the 18-yard box
- Great at finding short-and-long-distance passing lanes and excellent at passing the ball
- Can control the ball and dribble with pressure from many opponents
- Great endurance
- Communicates, acts, and leads as the coach on the field

Advantages:

- A team leader who directs the attack
- Plenty of opportunities for assists and to score goals
- Often one of the best dribblers on the team, with the freedom to travel wherever they feel they can help the team score

Disadvantages:

- With leadership comes responsibility, which means taking some of the blame for losses
- Often helps start the offensive play but does not always get the assist or goal
- Surrounded by many players from both teams, so they are constantly under pressure

Example Players:

Zinedine Zidane - Real Madrid and the French National Team. Zidane (also known as "Zizou") is arguably France's greatest soccer player ever. Although he is known as a bit of a hothead—especially after he headbutted a player in the World Cup Finals—he is a leader on his team and is beloved by many around the world. Zidane was born in the French coastal town of Marseille and was the son of Algerian immigrants. He started playing soccer in the alleys of a rough section of town. As a player, he went on to win the Ballon d'Or three times, the Champions League, the Euros, and even the World Cup—and these were only his on-the-field awards and trophies. He did the unimaginable by becoming Real Madrid's coach and won three straight Champions League titles—a feat that had never been accomplished before by a manager. He took a season off from coaching Real Madrid after winning the third trophy and is regarded by many to be the best all-around soccer star of all-time, considering his performances as both a player and coach.

"If you are determined and confident, there is nothing in this great existence that can stop you from achieving what you want."—Zinedine Zidane

Johan Cruyff – Barcelona, Ajax, and the Dutch National Team. Born in Amsterdam, Cruyff was very talented and hard-working from the start. At a young age, he was picked up by the Dutch powerhouse team, Ajax. Cruyff was the face behind the Netherlands' "Total Football," in which each player could play every position—and often did. Johan dazzled with his skills so much that he even has a skill named after him—the Cruyff. (See the third book in the *Understand Soccer* series, **Soccer Dribbling & Foot Skills: A Step-by-Step Guide on How to Dribble Past the Other Team**, for an in-depth explanation of how to perform this skill along with many other skills.

Additionally, it points out which skills that most players are taught that should be avoided.)

Cruyff has been named the Best Player in Europe, Footballer of the Year, and Top Scorer. Additionally, he is a Dutch and Spanish Champion who has won the UEFA Super Cup and Intercontinental Cup.

"You have got to shoot; otherwise, you cannot score."— Johan Cruyff

YouTube: If you would like to see a video on the attacking midfielder position, then consider watching the *Understand Soccer* YouTube video: *How to Play CAM in Soccer*.

Midfield Summary

Midfielders are the most versatile field players on the team. Due to their defensive and offensive roles, they must have skills in both departments to be effective. One area that makes a huge difference is their ability to move the ball from the defense to the offense. In the *Understand Soccer* series book, **Soccer Passing & Receiving: A Step-by-Step Guide on How to Work with Your Teammates**, the form for an inside-of-a-foot pass, among other topics, is broken down step-by-step, as follows:

1. Plant next to the ball, while pointing your foot and hips at your teammate

2. Keep your toe up, heel down, and ankle locked

3. Keep your knees slightly bent and foot slightly off the ground

4. Follow through after making contact with the ball

Additionally, a midfielder will find themselves surrounded by multiple opponents nearly the entire game. Therefore, midfielders must have a few effective foot skills that they are comfortable using to ensure that they can keep the ball safe. The following are the Tier 2 foot skills. To learn the Tier 1 foot skills, consider grabbing a copy of the *Understand Soccer* series book, **Soccer Dribbling & Foot Skills: A Step-by-Step Guide on How to Dribble Past the Other Team**, where the best skills for each game situation are revealed.

Tier 2 Foot Skills

| Scissor | Roll | Step Over |

Chapter 10

False Nine

Jersey Number: #9

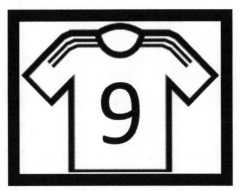

Understand that this is an uncommon role, and 99% of coaches will never use this position. However, it can be a huge benefit to a team that has an all-star player, or a team that cannot create enough space to score. A false nine is a soccer player who is positioned as a center forward. Since center forwards are often given the #9 jersey, this is where the "nine" in false nine comes from. The difference between a false nine and a center forward (i.e., a true nine) is that the false nine will play more like an attacking midfielder. This means they will drop deeper towards their net than a center forward would. This allows them to both open lanes for wingers to cut in and to help pull a defender off the defensive/back line.

Most teams will make sure that each of the opposing team's forwards/strikers are man-marked. Therefore, they will assign one specific defender to them. Thus, if a false nine acts more like an attacking midfielder, then it forces the defender to make a choice. The defender may either leave the back line, which will create space for the false nine's teammates, or they can stay at the back line, but this will increase the likelihood of no one covering the false nine.

Center forwards usually position themselves next to the deepest defender. By doing this, they can vertically stretch the pitch and spread the opposing team. This creates larger gaps, which increases the chance to score. The coach who implements a 4-4-2 formation (i.e., four defenders, four midfielders, and two forwards) with a striker and center forward, or two center forwards, is assuming that their forwards are better than the defenders who are covering them, thereby giving them the advantage to score.

The false nine is more commonly found in the Latin American and Spanish preferred 4-3-3 formation, in which there are four defenders, three midfielders, and three forwards. Using the false nine requires a very skilled player with considerable soccer intelligence, who has the vision to unlock space in the defense. Since a false nine is positioned as a "forward," they must still score goals, but they share goal-scoring responsibilities with wingers.

Skills Needed:

- Vision to pass around the opposition's defenders
- Fast reaction time
- Outstanding foot skills
- Can score
- Can pass well

Advantages:

- Creates havoc for the defense to determine who should mark them
- Accumulates many goals and assists over the course of a season
- Often the most technical player on the team

Disadvantages:

- Takes responsibility when their team does not score
- Must have the soccer intelligence to know when to drop into the midfield versus when to attack
- Since there is no obvious opposing player to mark them, they may be covered by two players at once, which is a disadvantage for the false nine as an individual but beneficial to the false nine's team

Example Players:

Francesco Totti - Roma and the Italian National Team. Although he does not have as many trophies as the other players in this book, he has a love for his team like no one else. Raised in Rome, he only dreamed of playing for Roma, and he ended up doing so for all of his senior career. Although Roma is a great team, it is outstanding that he did not chase money and trophies by transferring to a more prestigious team, yet still managed to win several trophies and awards, including the Top Scorer Award, Footballer of the Year, the European Under-21 Championship, and the World Cup. In Italy, he has won the Serie A, the Italian Cup, and the Italian Super Cup.

"Francesco Totti is impressive. He is an example for all, and someone we all look up to. He shows that age is not important in soccer. If you feel good, you enjoy it. If you play at the level he does, it is good for him, for soccer, and also for the children because we give them the idea that soccer has no limits."—Cristiano Ronaldo

Lionel Messi - Paris Saint-Germain, Barcelona, and the Argentinian National Team. Although Messi can play many roles—and he has—he is included as a false nine in this book because of his time under Pep Guardiola. Frankly, Messi can be placed in any attacking position and still be considered one of the greatest of all-time. At an early age, Messi was diagnosed with a growth hormone deficiency. At age 13, he moved from Argentina to Spain to play for Barcelona, in large part because they agreed to pay for his medical treatments. He quickly grew in their youth academy and made his senior team debut at 17 years old.

During the 2010-11 campaign, Pep Guardiola decided to use Lionel Messi as a false nine, similar to how the Roma coach, Luciano Spalletti, used Francesco Totti. Messi did not have the size or strength to use his body against the defenders like a traditional forward, but he was too good a player to not be centrally located on the field. Pep feared using him in the midfield because a designated player would mark him, and the midfield is the most congested portion of the field. This genius idea allowed Messi to lead the attack and win the coveted treble for Barcelona. Messi is one of the most decorated players of all-time. With multiple Ballon d'Ors, Best Player in Europe, Top Scorer, and Player of the Year, it is easy to see why he has so many fans. Aside from his personal achievements, this Olympian has also won several Champions Leagues, Spanish Championships, Spanish Cups, and Spanish Super Cups. Additionally, he has won the Club World Cup, the Under-20 World Cup, and the UEFA Super Cup.

"I start early, and I stay late, day after day, year after year. It took me 17 years and 114 days to become an overnight sensation."—Lionel Messi

YouTube: If you would like to see a video on the false nine position, then consider watching the *Understand Soccer* YouTube video: *False Nine*.

Chapter 11

Winger

Jersey Number: **Right Winger - #7**

Left Winger - #11

Note: These are the same numbers as the right midfielder and left midfielder.

Wingers aim to use their positioning to help increase the space between defenders. Wingers send crosses into the 18-yard box and finish them from the other winger on the opposite side of the field. Wingers attack the opponent's full backs and travel behind the defense, thereby making it easy to cross the ball towards the center for their attacking teammates to score.

Modern soccer is seeing a huge surge in wingers who dribble defenders and shoot. Since they play in the flanks, the wingers' opposition are usually the other team's full backs. Their role is like that of outside midfielders—except wingers play a bit farther up the field and are expected to score significantly more. Look at the image to further understand the difference in field positioning between an outside midfielder (i.e., left midfielder) and a winger (i.e., right winger).

Due to their increased role in producing goals, they are not always required to track back quickly to help their defenders.

Often, a team's winger is one of their fastest players on the field and covers the least crowded area of the field. Since they play in the less crowded flanks, they are expected to be great options to whom their teammates can pass the ball. In Latin and Dutch soccer countries, wingers usually play more like two outside forwards, as part of a 4-3-3 formation. However, the 4-4-2 is more prevalent in English-speaking countries, and the wingers are essentially the two outside midfielders.

Wingers generally function in one of two ways: Either they are an "out-and-out winger," or an "inside winger." The traditional winger is an out-and-out winger who positions themselves in the flanks. They use their speed to travel past the opposition's full backs, and they cross the ball to deliver solid passes to attacking teammates.

While many wingers prefer to stay out wide and travel in behind the full back, others act as an inverted/inside winger and dribble towards the net, either to pass a through ball to the striker or to shoot the ball themselves, often from outside the 18-yard box. Inverted wingers who want to cut in and shoot often line up on the side opposite their dominant foot. For example, if they are right-footed, then they take the position of a left winger to cut across the top of the 18-yard box to shoot. Many of the world's biggest clubs (e.g., Barcelona, Real Madrid, and Bayern Munich) play their wingers on the opposite side.

Both examples of players included at the end of this chapter are considered to be "inverted wingers" because the out-and-out winger is a dying breed. Talented wingers want to share goal-scoring and not only contribute via assists from crosses on the wings.

Skills Needed:

- Speed and agility
- Can cross the ball accurately
- Can dribble defenders
- Takes accurate shots from a distance
- Has a considerable amount of endurance
- Receives passes and quickly accelerates the ball up the field

Advantages:

- Quick and skilled at taking on players in 1v1 situations
- Can shoot the ball powerfully from outside the 18-yard box
- Has a considerable amount of space in the flanks

Disadvantages:

- Does not get as many touches because they are off to one side and often away from the play

- A considerable amount of running—especially when the coach expects them to track back on defense
- Sometimes expected to only play as out-and-out wingers and contribute crosses into the 18-yard box, leaving little room for taking shots themselves

Example Players:

Arjen Robben – Chelsea, Real Madrid, Bayern Munich, and the Dutch National Team. Robben is an inside winger who controls the right flank and creates enough room to cut in and shoot with his left foot. When many people think of Robben, they only think of his ability to cut in and shoot towards the far post, as this is how nearly all his goals are scored. Considered to be a "glass man" because of his injuries early in his career, Robben has traveled around many of the major European teams and won each specific country's league. He has done this in the Netherlands, Spain, England, and Germany. Additionally, he has a UEFA Super Cup to his name, as well as Player of the Year and Footballer of the Year in the leagues he competed in.

"The best thing about soccer—and sports in general—is that if you suffer a big disappointment, there is no better feeling than coming back the following year and doing well."—Arjen Robben

Cristiano Ronaldo - Juventus, Real Madrid, Manchester United, and the Portuguese National Team. Ronaldo is an inside winger who loves to play the left wing to cut in and shoot with his dangerous right foot. However, his versatile skillset allows him to play in any attacking position that he desires. Ronaldo's swift pace—coupled with his ability to shoot from a distance—makes him hard to cover. Additionally, he is effective at dribbling a defender—and even more effective at heading in the ball. When it comes to awards, Ronaldo is among the top 5 all-time players. It is hard to consider where to start when looking at his history of winning. He is a multiple Ballon d'Or winner, and roughly the 20X top scorer in his league throughout his career. He has numerous Super Cups, has won a handful of Champions Leagues, lifted the 2016 European Championship, and is a league winner in England, Spain, and Italy. Also, Ronaldo captained the first-ever team to win the UEFA Nations League Cup.

"Talent without working hard is nothing."—Cristiano Ronaldo

YouTube: If you would like to see a video on the winger position, then consider watching the *Understand Soccer* YouTube video: *Soccer Winger Movement*.

Chapter 12

Forward

Jersey Number: #9

Traditionally, center forwards were required to be tall and physically strong to win the ball. A center forward is often man-marked by at least one player and has two players covering them. Due to their large stature, they are often responsible for five main jobs: (1) receiving clearances, (2) holding the ball, (3) making passes to strikers and wingers, (4) poaching goals from headers, and (5) contributing powerful long-range strikes.

The terms "center forward" and "striker" are often used interchangeably. However, center forwards are really "second strikers," whose positioning is behind a striker. They are big physical presences, whereas strikers tend to be speedsters who can dribble past defenders with ease.

A forward who can control clearances will allow a team to boot the ball out of their defense because they know that their point man (i.e., the forward) can handle the ball. Kicking the ball over the midfielders will reduce the chance of mistakes—and will especially reduce the amount of time that the opposing team has to get into their defensive position. A forward needs to use their size to hold the ball, while wingers and midfielders travel up the field to assist the attack. Once the wingers, midfielders, and striker find enough space or make solid runs up the field, the forward will distribute the ball to players with more speed. Forwards use short and quick passes with movement off the ball to create openings for their team.

Most importantly, they are judged on their ability to score. Although they tend to obtain more assists than a striker, they are still expected to contribute many goals each season. Their size helps them score with their feet—and especially their head. Heading the ball with power and accuracy is a must because of how tall they are, compared to most other players on the field.

Forwards tend to fall into at least one of two categories: (1) clinical finishers, and/or (2) targets. Clinical finishers specialize in skills related to shooting with power from a distance. They are called "clinical" because they score on a high percentage of their shots and rarely hesitate to take an open shot. Clinical finishers can be recognized by the precise placement of their shots, as well as their high goals-to-shots ratio. The other type of forward is the "target," who receives the ball up the field and is great at distributing to faster teammates. This player serves as an outlet for the midfielders and defenders, who can hold the ball up to wait for support. Furthermore, targets can make runs to create enough space and open the field for other players, thereby allowing their teammates to dribble past fewer opposing players to score.

However, let us not forget that a forward's major role is to put goals in the net, and their performances are judged by results. Although they may help pressure the other team to create turnovers, they still need to score to be considered productive.

Skills Needed:

- Judging a ball while it is travelling in the air to control or head it
- Good movement to evade the opposition's center backs and create space
- Powerful, accurate headers
- Formidable size
- Accurate, powerful strikes
- Good passing skills
- Can win physical battles with defenders

Advantages:

- Minimal defensive responsibilities
- Their large physical presence commands respect from the other team's players
- Usually gets the glory when their team wins because they were involved in scoring

Disadvantages:

- Takes responsibility when the team cannot score
- May be benched—or even cut—if they experience an extended period without scoring
- Often covered by two defenders from the other team

Example Players:

Abby Wambach - Washington Freedom and the United States Women's National Team. Wambach is known for her goal-scoring ability. She was not the fastest or best on the ball, but she was physical and had a very direct style of play. Additionally, her stellar positioning allowed her to get onto the end of long balls and crosses. Her 5'11" physique allowed her to excel in the air. In her international career, Wambach scored 184 goals in 256 international matches. 77 of those goals were scored with her head. She is the leading all-time international scorer between both men and women.

In her freshman year with the University of Florida Gators, Abby led her team to their first NCAA National Championship over the 15-time champion North Carolina Tar Heels. Abby Wambach helped the Gators secure multiple titles. At the University of Florida, Wambach set school career records for goals, assists, points, game-winning goals, and hat tricks. Due to her successes in college, the United States Women's National Team recruited her. Throughout her career, she scored 184 goals—36 more than Mia Hamm, the next closest player. She even had one game in which she scored five goals. Abby has won a record six U.S. Soccer Female Player of the Year Awards, two Olympic Gold medals, and a World Cup title.

"I've never scored a goal in my life without getting a pass from someone else."—Abby Wambach

Zlatan Ibrahimović – LA Galaxy, Manchester United, Paris Saint-Germain, AC Milan, Barcelona, Inter Milan, Juventus, Ajax, and the Swedish National Team. Zlatan was born in Sweden to a Bosnian father and a Croatian mother. Therefore, he could have played for any of those three countries on the international stage. He chose to play for Sweden since he was born and raised there. He has two black belts in

Taekwondo, which explains many of his unusual ways of scoring, as well as his ability to kick his legs well over his head to strike the ball out of the air. His international career has seen him become Sweden's all-time leading scorer. Zlatan is such a huge national hero in Sweden that his name has been added to the Swedish Dictionary as a verb. The term "to Zlatan" means to dominate with extreme talent. With a bigger-than-life personality, Zlatan is known for his ability to score and his confidence.

Zlatan is a multiple-time Top Scorer, Player of the Year, and Footballer of the Year. He is a French, Spanish, Italian, and Dutch Champion, and he holds many cups in these countries. Even during a short stint in England, he produced an English League Cup, an English Super Cup, and a Europa League win. While Zlatan was playing for Manchester United, he was asked who he felt were the best strikers in the Premier League. He said, *"Sergio Agüero and Romelu Lukaku are the best strikers in the Premier League."* The reporter then asked Zlatan why he did not list himself, and Zlatan stated, *"Lions, they do not compare themselves to humans."* This type of bold self-confidence is often associated with forwards and strikers since these players are responsible for winning games via goals for their team.

YouTube: If you would like to see a video on the forward position, then consider watching the *Understand Soccer* YouTube video: _Soccer Forward Tactics_.

Chapter 13

Striker

Jersey Number: #9

Strikers are positioned in front of the forwards and are the players nearest the other team's goal. A striker's main job is to strike (i.e., score). Additionally, strikers tend to create many scoring chances for their teammates. Many players and coaches use the terms "striker" and "forward" interchangeably because their roles are similar.

The coaching staff may occasionally require one striker to play next to the last defender (often the sweeper) of the opposing team. Since most opposing coaches will have a center back or full back marking your team's striker, standing next to the sweeper means that there will be two defenders "marking" the striker. This will create significant gaps in the defense, thereby making it easier for teammates to score. Conversely, if the striker is the team's only chance of scoring, then the coach will often tell them to find enough space to receive the ball, which often means going back to the midfield, like a false nine.

Teammates will pass to the striker as often as possible. Given that a striker is normally a team's best goal-scorer, the other team will apply significant pressure to them. Therefore, a striker should be fast enough to collect long balls played by both midfielders and defenders, a forward who will stand with their back to the net and collect the soccer ball like a Target. Strikers should read the defense to find holes in which to receive passes and score tap-ins. Strikers should have a powerful and accurate shot to finish from anywhere in or around the 18-yard box. Furthermore, strikers need to dribble to avoid the outstretched defender's legs.

Strikers often make great counterattackers. Counterattackers are occasionally midfielders but mostly strikers, who use their speed to move the ball quickly up the field. A counterattack occurs when the soccer ball is dispossessed from the other team and is played either towards the counterattacking player or into space ahead of the counterattacking player. Since the other team is in an offensive shape when they have the ball, they are not yet set to defend correctly after losing possession of it. Counterattackers take advantage of the few seconds in which the other team is working to get into their correct defensive positions. Great shooting abilities will make counterattacking even easier.

Lastly, strikers may also contribute defensively by stealing the ball from defenders. When the other team's defense has the ball, strikers should strategically pressure the less skilled defenders, or the defenders with poor positioning, to increase their chance of winning back the ball. Excitingly, if the striker can steal the ball from a defender, then they will not have to beat very many players on the other team to score.

Skills Needed:

- Powerful, accurate shots
- Fast reaction time to recover rebounds
- Speed and agility
- Can dribble the ball and beat a defender
- Can control difficult passes
- Can score

Advantages:

- Receives praise often for wins because they are the ones to score
- Often, they are the player who is most looked up to by fans

- Can dribble, shoot, and score, which makes them the envy of most other players

Disadvantages:

- Takes responsibility when the team cannot score
- May be benched—or even cut—if they have an extended period without scoring
- Often covered by two defenders from the other team

Example Players:

Sergio Agüero - Manchester City, Atlético Madrid, and the Argentinian National Team. Agüero is widely known as "'Kun" because of his resemblance to a character in a Japanese cartoon show called "Kum-Kum the Little Caveman," which he watched and enjoyed as a child. He made a name for himself at a young age by winning the U-20 World Cup for Argentina. He helped Atlético Madrid earn a spot in the Champions League for the first time in 10 years when he played for them. Additionally, during his time at Manchester City, Agüero's last-minute goal at the end of the 2012 season won the Premier League title for Manchester City after a 44-year drought. Agüero is an EPL top scorer, English Champion, Olympian, FA Community Shield Holder, and Europa League winner.

"You have to know your limits, so you know how to push past them."—Sergio Agüero

Robert Lewandowski - Bayern Munich, Borussia Dortmund, and the Polish National Team. Lewandowski is a prolific scorer and rare find. To further understand the human body and increase his ability to train and gain strength, he obtained a bachelor's degree in Physical Education. On September 22, 2015, he broke four Guinness World Records as a Bayern Munich substitute in a game versus Wolfsburg by scoring five goals in nine minutes. Keep in mind that this is in the top German flight against a quality team. He has about 16 Top League Scorer titles and has won Footballer of the Year about 10 times. Lewandowski is a German and Polish Champion, a German and Polish Super Cup Winner, and the Captain of the Polish National Team.

"As a striker, you are playing against big defenders. They try to throw you around. I try to play in behind them, and I need power. I know that I have to go to the gym and train. I train all the time."—Robert Lewandowski

YouTube: If you would like to see a video on the striker position, then consider watching the *Understand Soccer* YouTube video: *Striker in Soccer*.

Attacking Summary

An attacking soccer player's main purpose is to score. Therefore, consider grabbing a copy of the *Understand Soccer* series book **Soccer Shooting & Finishing: A Step-by-Step Guide on How to Score**, to learn the various ways to strike a ball, how to win in 1v1s, 1v2s, 2v1s, and 2v2s, and how to increase your chances of scoring using easily remembered steps. Although there are various ways to shoot the ball, the most common shot is a driven shot, performed as follows:

1. Start diagonal to the ball.
2. Plant one foot away from the ball.
3. With the leg you are striking the ball with, keep your toe down and out, and your knee facing the net so that you can use the bone of your foot.
4. Follow through, land on your shooting foot, bring your back leg forward, and point your hips where you want to score.

Chapter 14

The Coach

Outfit: Suit or Tracksuit

The soccer coach is largely responsible for managing everyone and their expectations. A soccer coach reports upwards and downwards: upwards towards the owners and directors of the club and downwards towards the fans, staff, parents, and players. In professional leagues and national teams, the Head Coach is referred to as the "manager." In an amateur game (e.g., youth and college teams,) the term "coach" is used instead.

Being responsible for so many people requires good communication skills and the ability to balance many things at one time. Ultimately, for a coach, the best way to manage expectations and relationships with others is to win. At the end of the day, a coach is judged by their wins and losses. Therefore, the team's record will decide whether the coach will continue to have success at the club or will face their departure—potentially even before the season is done.

Coaches play a huge part in selecting the players on their team. Keep in mind that when they take their coaching position with a club, there are already many players on the team. The coach must then determine which ones they want to keep, and which ones they are willing to cut, loan, or sell. These actions require that expectations are managed to avoid reducing the team's feeling of security, while still removing any parts of the team that have significant room for improvement by bringing in quality players.

Furthermore, a coach determines the team's tactics that are used in a game, the formation on the pitch, and where each player lines up. Whether it be the Tiki-taka tactics used by Pep Guardiola, or the fluid changes in tactics implemented by Sir

Alex Ferguson, a coach needs to determine what play style will work best for their team. They must consider what type of soccer players are on their team, what each player can handle, and the fitness levels of each athlete to determine which formation would be best.

Lastly, knowing where to play each player based on their skills and abilities will help the team work together as one unit to win many titles, trophies, and awards. If you are a coach who is looking for drills with specific coaching points to use in practices that will increase your players' skills, then grab a copy of the *Understand Soccer* series book, **Soccer Drills: A Step-by-Step Guide on How to Coach the Perfect Practice**.

Skills Needed:

- Confident actions and tone of voice
- Leadership traits
- Willing to accept responsibility for losses and praise players for wins
- Determines which tactics best suit their team
- Understands what type of player best fits each position
- Can receive feedback well and does not get anxious before games or after losses
- Can manage the different players' personalities

Advantages:

- Responsible for all wins
- Significant influence with owners and directors
- Close to total control of players and staff
- Decides who sits and who plays, based on players' performance in previous games and efforts in practice

Disadvantages:

- Responsible for all losses
- Manages relationships and expectations of owners, directors, players, and staff
- Can be fired mid-season and without notice

Example Coaches:

Pep Guardiola - Manchester City, Bayern Munich, and Barcelona. As a former soccer player, Guardiola won 16 trophies with Barcelona during his playing career. Interestingly, he turned down Barcelona's first request to sign him. His enjoyable demeanor and wonderful tactics have allowed Pep to reach heights that few coaches have ever reached. Guardiola's first coaching success came with Barcelona, where he implemented his Tiki-taka style of play. Tiki-taka involves high probability/short passing. This helps the team keep possession of the ball and frustrate the opposition, who is given possession as little as 15% of the time. Invented by Johan Cruyff, Guardiola implemented it at Barcelona, using Xavi and Iniesta at the center of the scheme. Furthermore, Pep was the brains behind bringing Lionel Messi into a more central position, so he could get many more touches on the ball. In just five years at Barcelona, Guardiola won 14 major trophies that included four La Ligas, two Copa del Reys, two Spanish Super Cups, two Champions Leagues, two Super Cups, and two Club World Cups. This includes the highly coveted Treble in 2008-2009. Furthermore, Guardiola has won the World's Best Club Coach, Club World Cup, English League Cup, English Super Cup, and German Cup, and he became the Champion in Spain, Germany, and England.

"In soccer, the worst things are excuses. Excuses mean you cannot grow or move forward."—Pep Guardiola

Sir Alex Ferguson - Manchester United. Having won 24 trophies in 23 seasons, Alex Ferguson established himself as the most successful manager in English soccer history. After he won a treble for Manchester United, the queen knighted him. She was very appreciative for all his efforts to advance English soccer and bestowed this great honor upon him because of it. Unlike Pep Guardiola, who has a preferred play style, Sir Alex Ferguson is always willing to cut, add, move around, and refocus his team's tactics and formations. Similar to Pep Guardiola, Sir Alex Ferguson has several trophies and awards to his name. He was voted the World's Best Club Coach, and he won multiple Champions Leagues, English, and Scottish Championships, as well as Super Cups. He has won the Intercontinental Cup, FIFA Club World Cup, English FA Cup, English League Cup, and Scottish League Cup.

"For a player—and for any human being—there is nothing better than hearing, 'Well done.' Those are the two best words ever invented in sports. You don't need to use superlatives."—Sir Alex Ferguson

Coaching Summary

Coaches have a variety of roles in the organization, from selecting formations and game tactics to managing players' personalities and their parents. If you are interested in learning more about the coach's role, and its impact on the team, pick up a copy of the *Understand Soccer* series book, **Soccer Coaching: A Step-by-Step Guide on How to Lead Your Players, Manage Parents, and Select the Best Soccer Formation**. This book will help you learn what it takes to make players want to play for you, parents willing to work with you, and team positioning to fit your players' abilities. Here is an excerpt from the book about the 4-3-3 formation:

The 4-3-3 formation is all about maintaining possession and scoring many goals. Late in games, when a team is down by a goal or two, the coach will often change the formation to a 4-3-3 to increase the chance of producing a goal at the expense of giving up a midfield player because in most circumstances, the number of points that a team loses by does not matter. In the 4-3-3, the midfielders are located more centrally and work to clog the middle of the midfield and dispossess the other team. Once possession is won, the ball is played to the wingers and carried up the field's flanks.

The 4-3-3 uses two offensive wingers to either transport the ball up the flanks and cross it into the 18-yard box or cut in and strike the ball, like an inverted winger. The 4-3-3 also has two common variations: the 4-2-3-1, and the 4-3-2-1. Unsurprisingly, the 4-3-3 has had a tremendous impact on Spanish soccer, due to the hotbed of soccer talent that Spain has become.

Afterword

You may have noticed from the image at the beginning of the book of all the different possible positions that there was no chapter on the Inside Right or Inside Left positions. This was intentional because the modern game has basically eliminated these positions. Granted, there are some teams that will shift the forwards' play style to resemble some of the characteristics of the Inside Right or Inside Left. For example, Mohamed Salah of Liverpool and the Egyptian National Team is a right winger, who has minimal defensive responsibilities and is told to push towards the middle, similar to an Inside Right. Roberto Firmino will drop off from a center forward position and play more like an attacking center midfielder. This play style has also appeared at times while Cristiano Ronaldo and Karim Benzema were teammates at Real Madrid.

Therefore, the play style of an Inside Right or Inside Left is a blend of a winger and a forward. The W-M Formation, an early formation of many teams in soccer, heavily used the Inside Right and Inside Left, but it has been out of favor for nearly a century. However, it is important that you know what it is, in case someone ever mentions it.

Also, the tactics and formations used by a coach can change dramatically. Each position mentioned in this book may change a bit, based on the coach's style of play. A coach may even change the position of a player, or their team's formation during a game, so it is important to have some overlapping skills, and the knowledge of what is expected of each position.

This book is all about helping you determine where you fit best on a team, where each of your players should be positioned, and what skills are needed for you to perform in the position you have always wanted to play. This book was created to reveal the advantages and disadvantages of all the different positions. To fully develop the skills that each of the individual positions require, read the other technical books in the *Understand Soccer* series.

As a player or coach who wants to become better at playing or teaching soccer, remember that your ability to grow is often directly tied to the knowledge that you gain and implement. Consider reading the *Understand Soccer* series book, **Soccer Coaching; A Step-by-Step Guide on How to Lead Your Players, Manage Parents, and Select the Best Soccer Formation**. This book provides numerous examples of great formations to be used by coaches. The combination of knowledge found in *Soccer Positions* and *Soccer Coaching* details the abilities needed for each position, and where all the players should be appropriately placed in the team's formation.

As with anything in life, you will need to practice and experiment to find out what works best. Never stop growing and trying to better your understanding of the game. Remember that your ability on the field will grow in proportion to the knowledge you gain. Becoming a better coach or player cannot simply be done overnight by reading one book, so continue to improve your soccer education to make sure that you become the best player or coach you can be.

If you enjoyed this book, then please leave a review on Amazon to let me know.

WAIT!

Wouldn't it be nice to have the steps in this book on an easy one-page printout for you to take to the field? Well, here is your chance!

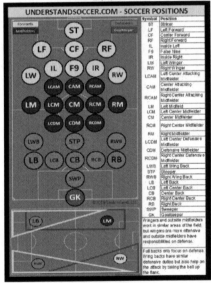

Go to this Link for an **Instant** One-Page Printout:
UnderstandSoccer.com/free-printout

This FREE guide is simply a thank you for purchasing this book. This one-page printout will ensure that the knowledge you obtain from this book makes it to the field.

About the Author

There he was—a soccer player who had difficulties scoring. He wanted to be the best on the field but lacked the confidence and knowledge to make his goal a reality. Every day, he dreamed about improving, but the average coaching he received, combined with his lack of knowledge, only left him feeling alone and unable to attain his goal. He was a quiet player, and his performance often went unnoticed.

This all changed after his junior year on the varsity soccer team of one of the largest high schools in the state. During the team and parent banquet at the end of the season, his coach decided to say something nice about each player. When it was his turn to receive praise, the only thing that could be said was that he had scored two goals that season—even though they were against a lousy team, so they didn't really count. It was a very painful statement that after the 20+ game season, all that could be said of his efforts were two goals that didn't count. One of his greatest fears came true; he was called out in front of his family and friends.

Since that moment, he was forever changed. He got serious. With a new soccer mentor, he focused on training to obtain the necessary skills, build his confidence, and become the goal-scorer that he'd always dreamed of being. The next season, after just a few months, he found himself moved up to the starting position of center midfielder and scored his first goal of the 26-game season in only the third game.

He continued with additional training led by a proven goal-scorer to build his knowledge. Fast-forward to the present day, and, as a result of the work he put in, and his focus on the necessary skills, he figured out how to become a goal-scorer who averages about two goals and an assist per game—all because he increased his understanding of how to play soccer. With the help of a soccer mentor, he took his game from being a bench-warmer who got called out in front of everybody to becoming the most confident player on the field.

Currently, he is a soccer trainer in Michigan, working for Next Level Training. He advanced through their rigorous program as a soccer player and was hired as a trainer. This program has allowed him to guide world-class soccer players for over a decade. He trains soccer players in formats ranging from one-hour classes to weeklong camps, and he instructs classes of all sizes, from groups of 30 soccer players all the way down to working one-on-one with individuals who want to play for the United States National Team.

If you enjoyed this book, then please leave a review.

Additional Books by Dylan Joseph Available on Amazon:

Soccer Training: A Step-by-Step Guide on 14 Topics for Intelligent Soccer Players, Coaches, and Parents

Soccer Shooting & Finishing: A Step-by-Step Guide on How to Score

Soccer Dribbling & Foot Skills: A Step-by-Step Guide on How to Dribble Past the Other Team

Soccer Passing & Receiving: A Step-by-Step Guide on How to Work with Your Teammates

Free Book!

How would you like to get a book of your choosing in the *Understand Soccer* series for free?

Join the Soccer Squad Book Team today and receive your next book (and potentially future books) for FREE.

Signing up is easy and does not cost anything.

Check out this website for more information:

UnderstandSoccer.com/soccer-squad-book-team

Thank You for Reading!

Dear Reader,

I hope you enjoyed and learned from **Soccer Positions**. I truly enjoyed writing these steps and tips to ensure that you improve your game, your team's game, or your child's game.

As an author, I love feedback. Candidly, you are the reason that I wrote this book and plan to write more. Therefore, tell me what you liked, what you loved, and what can be improved! I'd love to hear from you. Visit UnderstandSoccer.com and scroll to the bottom of the homepage to leave me a message in the contact section or email me at:

Dylan@UnderstandSoccer.com

Finally, I need to ask a favor. **I'd love and truly appreciate a review.**

As you likely know, reviews are a key part of my process to see whether you, the reader, enjoyed my book. Your reviews allow me to write more books. Please take two minutes to leave a review on Amazon.com at:

https://www.amazon.com/gp/product-review/B07TRJ2J8G

In gratitude,

Dylan Joseph

Glossary

Note: In this glossary, the term "football" is used interchangeably with the term "soccer." Soccer is the name of the game in countries like the United States, Canada, and Australia. Football is used in Europe, the Middle East, South America, and Africa.

Back Line - The defenders on a soccer team forming the line in front of the goalkeeper.

Brazilian League Champion - The team in the Brasileirão Serie A with the most points after their 38 games of top-flight soccer in Brazil.

Champions League - A tournament of qualifying teams in Europe held yearly to determine who is considered the world's best club team (the European Champion). Often considered one of the top two trophies that every soccer player dreams of winning (the other being the World Cup).

CONCACAF Cup - A soccer competition to determine CONCACAF's entry into the FIFA Confederations Cup.

Confederations Cup - An annual African club team competition. Clubs qualify for it based on their performance in their cup competitions and national leagues.

Copa América - Known as the America Cup. This is an international men's soccer competition between national teams from South America. Since 1990, there have also been teams from North America and Asia invited to participate.

Counterattack (i.e., "Fast Break") - When the defending team gains possession of the ball and quickly moves the ball up the field with the objective of taking a quick shot, so few of the other team's players will have time to travel back to defend.

Croatian Cup - The Hrvatski Nogometni Kup is a club soccer tournament in Croatia. The winner qualifies for the UEFA Europa League.

Croatian League Champion - The team in the Croatian First Football League with the most points after their 34 games of top-flight soccer in Croatia.

Defender of the Year - Awarded to the player deemed the best defender in their domestic league.

Dutch Cup - Known as the KNVB Cup. This club competition is amongst the top 3 flights of soccer teams in the Netherlands along with 24 other qualifying teams from lower divisions.

Dutch League Champion - The team in the Eredivisie with the most points after their 34 games of top-flight soccer in the Netherlands.

Dutch Super Cup - Known as the Johan Cruyff Shield in the Netherlands and is played by the winner of the Eredivisie (Dutch league) and the winner of the national KNVB (Dutch) Cup. If the same team wins the Eredivisie and the KNVB Cup, then that team faces the runner-up in the national league.

English FA Cup - English club soccer competition that is the oldest national soccer competition in the world. It is run by The Football Association.

English League Champion - The team in the English Premier League with the most points after their 38 games of top-flight soccer largely in England.

English League Cup - English club soccer competition set up by the English Football League. The 92 teams of the top four levels of English soccer battle for this cup.

FA Community Shield - English contest between the champions of the Premier League and the winners of the FA

Cup. In the event that they are the same team, they will play the runner-up in the league instead.

FIFA Ballon d'Or - The premier individual soccer award based on votes from international journalists and national team coaches and captains. These sources select the player who performed the best in the previous calendar year.

FIFA Club World Cup - An international men's soccer tournament, which is supposed to determine what team is the best club in the world. However, it struggles to attract interest in most of Europe and is not considered a premier trophy due to the relative strength of clubs in Europe and South America compared to the rest of the world.

FIFA Under-20 World Cup - A soccer world championship between countries occurring every two years for male players under the age of 20. Before 2006, it was known as the FIFA World Youth Championship.

Flank - The right or left sides of the field closest to the sidelines.

Footballer of the Year - Presented by the Football Writers' Association, this is an award given to the player who is voted to have the most outstanding season in English soccer that year. The winner is voted on by around 400 soccer journalists based throughout England.

French Cup - The Coupe de France is a French club competition run by the French Football Federation. It is open to all amateur and professional soccer clubs in France (roughly 8,500 teams), including clubs based in the overseas territories.

French League Champion - The team in the Ligue 1 with the most points after their 38 games of top-flight soccer in France.

French League Cup - The Coupe de la Ligue is a French club competition run by the Ligue de Football Professionnel. The tournament is only open to professional clubs in France that play in the country's top three soccer divisions.

French Super Cup - The Trophée des Champions is a French soccer trophy awarded to the winner of the match between the winners of the Coupe de France and the champions of Ligue 1.

German Cup - Known as the DFB-Pokal Cup. This German soccer competition is held by the German Football Association where sixty-four club teams compete. It is considered the second-most important club title in German soccer after the Bundesliga championship.

German League Champion - The team in the Bundesliga with the most points after their 34 games of top-flight soccer in Germany.

German Super Cup - A German soccer match where the winners of the Bundesliga and the German Cup compete. It is run by the Deutsche Fußball Liga and if one team wins the Bundesliga and German Cup, they play the runner-up of the Bundesliga.

Intercontinental Cup - This is also referred to as the European/South American Cup. This was an official international soccer competition endorsed by UEFA and CONMEBOL between the winners of the UEFA Champions League and the South American Copa Libertadores. The competition has been replaced by the FIFA Club World Cup.

Italian Cup - The Coppa Italia is a club knockout competition in Italy. The winner qualifies for the UEFA Europa League group stage and the Supercoppa Italiana.

Italian League Champion - The team in the Serie A with the most points after their 38 games of top-flight soccer in Italy.

Italian Super Cup - An Italian soccer game played by the winners of the Serie A and the Italian Cup. If the winner of the Serie A and the Italian Cup are the same team, then they will play the Italian Cup runner-up.

MLS Cup Champion - The post-season championship game of Major League Soccer in the United States of America. This champion differs from other top soccer leagues around the world, which consider the club with the most points at the end of the regular season to be called the champion. The winner is crowned champion similar to other U.S.A. sports leagues through a playoff following a regular season.

MLS League Champion - The team in the MLS with the most points after their 34 games of top-flight soccer in the United States of America.

Olympic Medalist - A gold, silver, or bronze medal is awarded to successful players at the international stage during the Olympics every four years.

Player of the Year - The player voted as the best in their respective country's domestic soccer league that year.

Scottish Cup - A Scottish club soccer competition for all 90 clubs of the Scottish Football Association, along with up to eight other clubs who are associate members. The Scottish Cup trophy is the oldest national trophy in the world.

Scottish League Champion - The team in the Scottish Premiership with the most points after their season of top-flight soccer in Scotland.

Scottish League Cup - Soccer competition for Scottish Professional Football League teams. The competition used to have a straight knockout format but was then changed into a group and knockout competition.

Spanish Cup - Also known as the "Copa Del Rey," this club competition is among 83 teams from Spain's top four flights. This is the oldest soccer competition in Spain.

Spanish League Champion - The team in La Liga with the most points after their 38 games of top-flight soccer in Spain.

Spanish Super Cup - This is known as the Supercopa de España. This contest is for Spanish soccer teams competed for by the winners of La Liga and the Copa del Rey. If the winner of La Liga and the Copa del Rey are the same team, then the winner of La Liga will play against the runner-up of the Copa del Rey.

Top Scorer - The soccer player who scored the most goals in their domestic league.

Treble - Achieved when a club soccer team wins three trophies in a single season. A continental treble is earned by winning the club's national league competition, the national cup competition, and a continental trophy. A domestic treble is when a team wins three national competitions. Competitions which comprise a single match (e.g., the FA Community Shield, Irish FA Charity Shield, Supercopa de España, Trophée des Champions, the Recopa Sudamericana, the UEFA Super Cup, or the Intercontinental Cup) do not count towards a treble.

UEFA Best Player in Europe - Known currently as the UEFA Men's Player of the Year Award. This soccer award is given to a soccer player on a team in Europe. Performances at the club level and for their national team are considered. UEFA created the award in 2011 to revive the Ballon d'Or, which merged with the FIFA World Player of the Year Award in 2010 to become the FIFA Ballon d'Or. This award replaced the UEFA Club Footballer of the Year award.

UEFA Europa League - Previously called the "UEFA Cup," this is a soccer club competition for eligible European soccer clubs. Clubs earn a place in the competition based on their performance in their national leagues and cup competitions. It ranks below the UEFA Champions League.

UEFA European Under-21 Champion - A soccer competition for men on European teams under the age of 21. This competition is held every two years.

UEFA Super Cup - A match between the UEFA Champions League and the UEFA Europa League champions.

World Cup - A tournament of 32 qualifying nations from all over the world held every four years to determine which nation has the best soccer team. Often considered one of the top two trophies that every soccer player dreams of winning, the other being the Champions League.

World's Best Club Coach - Soccer award given to the most deserving club coach, as voted by the International Federation of Football History & Statistics.

Acknowledgments

I would like to thank you, the reader. I am grateful for the opportunity to provide you with value and to help you on your journey to become a more confident soccer player, coach, or parent. I am happy to serve you, and I thank you for the opportunity to do so.

Also, I would like to recognize people who have made a difference and paved the way for me to share this book with you:

I want to thank the grammar editors, Kimberly Stewart, Paul Marvar, and Abbey Decker. Their keen eyes ensured that the wording needed to convey the messages was appropriate, and they provided countless grammatical improvements.

Also, I would like to thank the content editors: Kevin Solorio, Toni Sinistaj, and Youssef Hodroj. They reviewed this book for areas that could be improved and suggested additional insights to share. Without their input, this book would not be the high-quality reading material that you have come to expect from the *Understand Soccer* series.

Many thanks,

Dylan Joseph

Made in the USA
Monee, IL
17 February 2022

91379298R00070